W9-ABI-046

Living Love

Living Love

*Meditations on the
New Testament*

RUTH BURROWS

Illustrated by ELIZABETH RUTH OBBARD

Dimension Books Inc.
Denville, N.J. 07834

242.1
B

First U.S.A. edition by Dimension Books Inc.
P.O. Box 811, Denville, N.J. 07834 through
arrangement with Darton, Longman and Todd Ltd, London

© 1985 Ruth Burrows

Illustrations © 1985
Elizabeth Ruth Obbard

ISBN 0–87193–243–1
All rights reserved

Phototypeset by
Input Typesetting Ltd,
London SW19 8DR
Printed in Great Britain by
Anchor Brendon Ltd, Tiptree, Essex

Contents

With Jesus in his Passion

Note

These short meditations were originally delivered orally during the course of the Lenten Office as reflections on some point of the day's liturgical texts. The author had only her Carmelite community in mind when she spoke, but it seemed to several people that a wider audience might benefit from her insights.

My thanks to Sister Bernadette of Newry Carmel who so generously undertook the preliminary editorial work, and of course to Ruth Burrows for allowing me to arrange and adapt her community talks for a more general readership. My warm thanks, too, to Sister Wendy Beckett for the Marantha on the last page and for inspiration with some of the translations from the Bible.

The majority of the scriptural quotations are taken from *The Jerusalem Bible*, published and copyright 1966, 1967 and 1968 by Darton, Longman and Todd Ltd and Doubleday & Co. Inc., by permission of the publishers.

ELIZABETH RUTH OBBARD
Editor

Jesu, were you nothing but a memory
How fragrant would that memory be!
But O, you are my living Love,
Sweetness itself, my life's delight.

Music of unearthly timbre
Of soaring joy no human ear can catch.
Beauty, beyond the frontiers of thought
Jesu, God's dear and holy Son.

('Jesu dulcis memoria', trans. R.B.)

Leaning on the Lord

Friend of Jesus

I call you friends.
(John 15:15)

Jesus calls us friends insofar as we go to him, cling to him, hang onto his words, scrutinize his deeds, his attitudes, his sense of values, in order to know the Father and do his will.

To be a friend of Jesus is to have as our sole reason for living the accomplishment of the Father's will in us and through us. This is the way Jesus was.

Jesus is our Way because he refused to have any way of his own except what the Father ordained for him; our Truth because he did not stand on anything as coming from himself but only as shown him by the Father; our Life because he was utterly selfless, an emptiness for the Father's love.

Nearly everyone (perhaps we have to say 'everyone', at least to begin with), in setting out to climb the mountain to meet God, is really after something for self. In so far as our poor, blind seeking is genuine, God is able to work to purify our motivation. This must cost us bitterly.

A fundamental resolution which, if we can hold on to it hour after hour, will leave us completely open to him and certain of our goal, is simply that God shall have all, everything he asks moment by moment.

Nothing shall matter to me any more. I have ceased to be important to myself.

I stay rooted in the heart of Jesus, drawing on the endless resources of my Way, Truth and Life – my Friend. He is steadfastly loyal to me; and on my side I must never let him down. This is possible only when I live in his heart and let him share his Father with me. This is 'leaning on the Beloved'.

Christom our Sun

**God so loved the world that he gave up his own Son . . .
for us**.   (cf. John 3:16)

These familiar words may have no impact on our minds
or imaginations. Rather, as some of us confronted with
the size and distance of stars remain untouched, so these
words mirror a knowledge beyond the range of our
faculties.

Are they then to remain dead? To drop like a stone on
a frozen lake, leaving the water beneath undisturbed?
No.

We are dealing with a God ever present to our deepest
selves. Though the mind cannot compass him, he can
encompass us, touch our deepest centre, so that we can
act out in our daily, hourly lives, our faith in this
absolute love of God, and his commitment to us.

God so loved the world . . . For the exceeding great
love God had towards us – when we had put ourselves
far, far, far away from him and were trapped, morose,
dying a dead death –
He came to us,
     stooped to us,
     caught us up in the living heart of his Son,
     healed our crookedness,
     unwound our bonds,
transformed our despair into joyful hope and praise.

The cry is still echoing: 'Arise you sleepy ones! You are still only half awake! Christ is shining on you like the newly risen sun, summoning you from death to the very fullness of life in him!'

Once knowledge of God's exceeding love becomes real knowledge – part of my very being – then there will be no stopping me.

Exceeding love will drive me on to give myself totally to God and my neighbour.

The Surrendered One

I am testifying on my own behalf.
(John 8:14)

'I am my own testimony . . .' for anyone with eyes
   to see.
Jesus alone can say this.
O peerless life of surrendered love!

And he can say it only because the Father enabled him
to become what he is.

> In him
> is the fullness of God
> giving himself to man,
> and the fullness of man
> offering himself to God.

In Jesus there was never any gap between what he was
and what he should have been. With us there always
is.

But if we really accept Jesus, really surrender to him,
make him our way, truth, life, our only holiness, then
the gap in us is closed and the Father can bear testimony
to us also:

> 'My son, my beloved.'

I Die Daily

No one takes my life, I lay it down of my own free will.
(John 10:18)

'I lay down my life of my own free will,' says Jesus, with humble pride. No one takes it from me, I give it. And the Father's answer to this act of blind trust and love is – Resurrection, glorification.

Jesus' actual physical death was the perfect summing up, the consummation, of a death he had accepted from the first and which had been going on throughout his earthly life.

So it is with us. Our final, supreme act of love and trust is the acceptance of final dissolution, but this will have only the intensity and reality of our daily acceptance of death.

We fight against this dying with every fibre of our natural being. When Jesus says he has power to lay down his life he is meaning that the Father empowers him to do it, for over and over again he stresses that he has no power of his own, no will of his own.

In our turn we know that we have no power of ourselves to accept death. Yet as Jesus is empowered by the Father and is utterly certain of this enablement because the Father has asked him to do as he does, so we are utterly certain of being able to accept to die daily in the power we draw from Jesus' own surrender.

We can never accept it of ourselves, it runs so counter to what we naturally want; but in the surrender that flows from Jesus we can.

The tiniest blow to self and we jump to defend that self, ward off the attack – be it against our comfort, our convenience, our self-image, our reputation, our security . . . If we don't succeed we submit passively because we have no alternative. But this is not what Jesus asks of us – 'I *lay it down* of my own free will.'

If only we could live our days with that written on our hearts, so that when death knocks in one way or another we instinctively accept; 'I *choose* to let it go . . . I give it away.'

As the Father found supreme joy in Jesus for the freedom he gave him to act in him with power, so he will find joy in us. 'My Father loves me because I lay down my life day by day, hour by hour.' Were there no promise . . . 'I take it again, a new, full life' . . . surely just being a joy to the Father in this way would be reward enough. Jesus would have thought so.

But the Father would never ask for useless sacrifice. The Father seeks only to love us to the end, to the uttermost fullness of love. If he asks us to die it can only be that we may receive the very fullness of life.

Chosen and Redeemed

It has pleased your Father to give you the kingdom.
(Luke 12:32)

The heart of Christianity is the wonderful fact that we are already redeemed. It has all been done for us. Now, we find this almost impossible to believe.

Our problem is that we are bedevilled with the notion that we have to do it all ourselves. We come to a knowledge of our wretchedness, of the evil deep within us. We find ourselves in such a disgusting mess that the conclusion is drawn:

> it's hopeless,
> I'm so bad,
> I'm not a good Christian.

I'm a hypocrite even being in the church and going through the motions!

This is all wrong, says Jesus. Just because you are like that, provided you cling to me, believe in me, honour me by blind trust, I can do *everything* for you, transform you into myself.

To believe this is to believe in the true God, the God who really is, the God Jesus reveals as Father, and who wants nothing from us but trust.

He is there with his arms outspread, eagerly awaiting our going to him. There is nothing to delay or hinder us —

only believe,
go to him,
cling to him,
never leave,
believe utterly in his power and will to save.

Then I can do all things in him who strengthens me.
With Jesus I can consent to lay down my life for love
of this Father; sure that he enables me to do so by
infusing his life within me.

It has pleased your Father to give you the kingdom.

Gift of the Father

The Father himself loves you.
(John 16:27)

His own Son is the Father's gift to us, and we must creep into that Son's welcoming heart, content to shelter in his holiness, his goodness, his wisdom.

There is no place for human pride in the presence of God.

We have no holiness, goodness or wisdom of our own. So to be made consciously aware that we are spiritually inadequate, faulty, wretched – that we fail and sin – is a precious grace.

Pride would make us angry with ourselves, or discouraged. Or on the other hand it might come into play further back and not allow us to become aware of our failings. It would provide us with the knack of sweeping them under the carpet, so we didn't have to face them.

Christian humility quietly faces up to all this without anger or discouragement. It calls to mind that there is One who always did his Father's will; who offers the Father perfect love and worship. And this One is the Father's gift to us.

From the shelter of the Son's heart we go on trying, with him, to do always what pleases the Father; but at the same time never wanting to feel we are becoming holy and good, without spot or wrinkle.

Never are we more truly in Christ Jesus than when, deeply conscious of our sinfulness, we peacefully rest in the heart of our Redeemer – the Risen One.

Sacrificial Love

The Father, who is the source of life.
(John 5:26)

The Father has given to Jesus his own prerogative of giving life. He has also given him the right to judge because he is the Son of Man.

In the Gospel of John the title, Son of Man, always denotes the sacrificed one, the holy Lamb. And it is because Jesus is the slain Lamb that he has the power and right to judge.

Why is this so?
This Lamb opened not his mouth. There was in him no element of evil.
He stood before us who found him worthy of annihilation.
We oppressed him.
We killed him.
Our evil found nothing in him as ally – not the least stirring of retaliation, only immense pity and love.

The Father returns him to us in Resurrection – as our judge. And how does he judge us?

The Risen Jesus has only one message: absolute forgiveness, total acceptance, total gift of himself to us if only we receive him. This is judgement. And behind Jesus stands the Father.

Jesus tells us that he is only acting out of his Father's heart, his Father's will. Jesus has no self-drives, he is pure receptacle for the Father's revelation and will.

Thus Jesus – infinite pity, forgiveness, acceptance, is a revelation of the Father: 'You alone can heal me *because* you my sins have grieved.'

How different, how utterly different, from our own ideas of justice!

Growth to Maturity

You must be born from above.
(John 3:7)

To 'be born from above': this demands a listening ear, a disciple's ear. Each morning he wakes me to hear, to listen like a disciple.

We are not born full men and women. We are born members of the human race and given the command to *become* man, to *become* woman. This is our primary life-task.

It is not automatic. It is not inevitable. It means following the example of Jesus' patience, his endurance; accepting the Cross. There is no becoming man without this.

To be woman or to be man means living outside myself, emptied, obedient, given away to others, wholly sacrificed, enduring all things in love. It means being governed by the will of God in duty and service to others, and not by my own wishes, emotions, ups and downs, whims, insecurities, compulsions. This selflessness can only be attained by bitter struggle, and in this Jesus gives us the example.

This is how Jesus lived, this is how he became man – by always listening to his Father, by having ears for nothing else but to know the Father's will and fulfil it, no matter what the cost.

We can truly say that the mystery of the Cross is the mystery of Jesus becoming Man, man in his truth and fullness. Jesus was perfected as Man in his death and resurrection.

We are Jesus' disciples and we must hang on his words, resolutely determined to have no other aim in life than the perfect fulfilment of the Father's will . . . I set my face like flint . . . I shall not be moved . . . by his help.

Jesus our Brother

My son, you are with me always and all I have is yours.
(Luke 15:31)

In the parable of the prodigal son these are the words of the father addressed to his mean firstborn.

Let us read them as the Father addressing his selfless, utterly loving Firstborn: 'My Son, you are always with me and everything I have is yours'.

In the Gospel of John Jesus affirms this – 'all you have is mine and all I have is yours, especially the men and women you have given me.' This Gospel celebrates the mutual joy the Father and the Son have in us; their delight in the great work of redemption; the joy that is in heaven because we are brought back to the Father, brought back to life in Christ.

'It was only right we should rejoice, because *your brother* here was dead and has come to life; he was lost and is found.'

How tender and beautiful the words of the Father to Jesus, 'your brother'. What a joy for us to be considered thus!

The Way of Discipleship

Light in the Lord

Anyone who follows me will not be walking in the dark.
(John 8:12)

From the start of our spiritual journey we are handi-capped. Our disorders blind us. And if we are blinded by our disorders it means we aren't going to realize how disordered we are. We may well think that we are mortified, that we *do* live for God alone. This com-placency is the effect of our blindness.

How on earth are we to break out of this vicious circle? We are blind so we don't realize that our appetites are running after selfish ends, and the more we run after them the blinder we become.

The ultimate answer is Jesus Christ our Lord, who has broken the trap.

But we don't see how we fail to follow his teaching; that again is part of our blindness. We follow him in a rough and ready sort of way, but not in that 'perfect' way he expects of us.

However, he is always pouring his light into us. He helps us to see what, unaided, we cannot see. He is always trying to stir our will to greater love. If we respond and earnestly want his light we shall get it.

Jesus does not force his light on us. We have to let him in with his flashlight; and we must really *want* to see.

So I invite you to open your door and let him in. Let him hold up his torch in your little chamber and reveal the cobwebs, spiders and dusty little idols. Let his torch scan your inner selves.

Let us ask if we are wholly and unreservedly living for God? Or do we allow ourselves to listen to the first whisperings of evil, of resentment, of anger against another? Do we give way to curious, interfering reflections on our neighbours . . . to doubt, anxiety, depression, scruples and so forth?

The all-important moment is the first one. Resist the first attack and we have conquered: give in and the whole thing gathers momentum, blinds us, overwhelms us.

We must cling to God as survivors to a spar, cling desperately, never letting go. And we can be sure that he will prove a rock to us, a rock that is not only steady under our feet, but that hides us from evil.

Being For-God

They put honour from men before the honour that comes from God. (John 12:43)

Our enslavement to human respect! Human respect is allowing the opinion of men to be more important than the truth of God.

We have to try to stand always before our Lord, to act in perfect truth before him and before men – and take the consequences. We must be free of human respect so that we can keep the gaze of our hearts on God alone.

But think what we do. We perhaps blunder and find it so hard to admit simply – we want to hide it, modify its proportions. We are shy about asking for something we want – we camouflage it, go beating round the bush. What an impediment this is!

On the whole we are quite ready to speak disparagingly of ourselves, but not too happy when others do so. And that's the real test of genuineness: 'Think little of yourself . . . and endeavour that others do likewise.' (John of the Cross)

There is a universal subservience to human respect. It is something *so* universal, operating nearly all the time, that unless we are shown it we do not see it, at least in its more subtle forms.

We crave to be somebody, to be important, to get a feel of ourselves as mattering. Of course we matter, absolutely, to God – but this isn't what we want! We want an importance flowing from our own self, our own worth and merits. Our natural being claims independence, a right to fulfilment.

But man's essence, man's true being, is a 'for-God-ness'. This actually constitutes a human being. It is not something added to my being, not a part of my human reality – it is the whole of me. My very being is a self-communication of God; the measure of my being is the measure of God's self-communication to me.

The more fully God communicates himself to me (and this depends on me), the more fully I am.

I am fully when God has been allowed to give himself to me to the extent of my capacity. This is union with God.

Jesus is the One in whom this self-communication of God was plenary, 'in him dwells all the fullness of God . . .' and it is for this reason we can say he is God. We can say he is God only because he is fully man – all his potential for-God-ness was activated and fulfilled.

Understanding this fundamental truth of man's being we can work more speedily and thoroughly at our reorientation towards God alone.

However, my natural being, which is what I experience of myself, rejects all this. So to affirm my absolute for-God-ness in practice calls for the leap of faith, and utmost generosity based on faith.

To live in continual affirmation of my true being calls for self-denial. I must not put honour from men before the honour that comes from God.

Alert and Alive

Blessed are those servants if he finds them alert.
(Luke 12:38)

'I want to be on the alert for our Lord, determined to take no notice of myself, of whether I am happy or not, suffering or not.' The cultivation of this attitude is necessary if we want to belong wholly to God. We must learn to ignore our emotional states. How important this is, and how few grasp it!

Feelings are important and play an enormous part in our maturing as human beings, but only when they are controlled, made to serve, not dominate us. Unless we are fully alert to this fact and have determined to get control of our emotional life we fall into all sorts of wrong thinking and doing.

Our range of needs, of wants, is vast. Beginning with our lower needs – how our feelings can change with the weather! Given a beautiful spring morning worries drop off us, for a while we feel bright and happy. If we are chilled to the bone, hungry, how readily we feel miserable. If we think we are well-liked, are successful, we feel gay and confident. If we think we are not appreciated we feel unhappy. When we have interesting work that engages our creativity we feel full of joy; when we have to go on day after day with monotonous, dull work, we can feel depressed. The list is endless – and what is said here is surely obvious.

What is not obvious is how easily we fail to recognize how these changing states of feeling, these drives for immediate satisfaction of one kind or another, and dread of the opposite, rule us. They dictate and govern our judgements, decisions, actions . . .

How common it is for our estimation of people to rest on how we 'feel' about them. In some way they please us, we understand their type and we judge them favourably. Whereas someone who makes us feel uneasy, isn't like us, seems to slight us, put us in the shade, or threatens us in some way, is judged unfavourably. The same happens with events.

It is not at all easy for us to stand back absolutely from ourselves and judge people and events as they are. (And we can never do this *absolutely* – one of the reasons why we must never presume to judge others.)

How often we hear complaints: 'I can't pray; I can't believe God loves me; life seems empty . . .' All that is being said is that the emotional state is painful, contrary to what we want.

We have to learn to live by our faith not by our emotions. Unless we do this we can never become truly spiritual, we can never be liberated from the tyranny of self.

A Heart of Compassion

Be compassionate as your Father is compassionate.
(Luke 6:36)

God is the author of all tender-heartedness and goodness.

Misericors – a heart always inclined to another in compassion, a pitiful heart. A heart that is always good – that is, wishing good to another. Wherever we meet these qualities, there, we can be sure, is God.

We have to be perfect as our Father is perfect, and especially as he is perfect in these qualities.

Let me look at my heart. Is it unfailingly tender towards others? Unfailingly bent on their good? Or do I see that there is a lot of hardness there?

Am I perhaps kind to some, but not to others? Kind at sometimes but not always? Not when I am upset, put-out, hurt . . . ? Do I wish well to others only when their good doesn't conflict with what I think is mine?

God is the fount of tender-heartedness and goodness. Ask him for the grace to drink deeply of this fountain. Want these God-like qualities with all your heart. Seize the opportunities each day offers to exercise them, no matter how much it costs pride and self-interest.

The Work of Faith

Work for your salvation 'in fear and trembling'.
(Philippians 2:12)

To work at a resolution never to murmur or complain, is a practical way of co-operating with the Father. Whatever he asks me to bear, I can bear with him. Complaints, even interior ones, mean I am not looking at him, my Father, who has infinite care of me.

'Work with fear and trembling.' What earnestness this suggests, what anxiety – of the right kind – to do his will; what an awareness that we are weak and blind, and have no ability as from ourselves to cope with life, to really give ourselves.

This 'fear and trembling' is nevertheless underpinned with a marvellous confidence. God himself is at work in us. He is giving us the desire to please him, and he will enable us to do so.

We must hold these two strands together:
1. A profound awareness of God and the demands he must make on us – utterly beyond our unaided strength; together with:
2. Absolute confidence that all things are possible with him. The impossible is actually possible. Rarely are these two strands held adequately together.

On the one hand we may *feel* confident, but it is only because we haven't faced up to the all-ness of God's demands, and so aren't unduly troubled.

On the other hand, having glimpsed something of them, we lack confidence in him. We think we have to do it by ourselves.

The result is, we never fling ourselves in; we continue to just sit on the bank and dangle our feet.

One with Christ

Can you drink the cup that I am going to drink?
(Matthew 20:22)

Union with Jesus consists not in sitting in glory but in sharing his cup of shame, opprobrium, dishonour and powerlessness. These are the things in his mind when he offers us his cup, not the physical sufferings of his passion.

How can we share this cup in our daily life?

By renouncing all power and every desire for it, every manoeuvre to obtain what we want, to prevail over others;

by taking an attitude of unimportance and subjection to the community;

by rejecting the right to insist on our rights;

by sacrificing the image we have of ourselves and which we sensitively want upheld in our own eyes and that of others;

renouncing all desire for status, of being important to others.

The cup Jesus wants to share with us is that of selfless love, which is its own reward – he offers no other.

We think we know what the chalice contains and express our eagerness to drink it. When it comes to the point, when it comes to drinking the above bitter ingredients, we turn away from it with loathing.

Heart and Flesh

With desire I have desired.
(Luke 22:15)

If we would be all God's we must admit only one desire; that of pleasing our Father.

He cannot be had just for the asking. It calls for a lifetime of effort – sustained effort. It is worked out in our daily life.

We chasten, discipline, control our bodiliness (which is none other than ourself) in relation to everything and everyone around us, which and whom we can contact only through our bodies.

This is so that our hearts burn with one single pure desire – for God.

'I give Christ my body to make up what is still to be suffered, the pain he must still endure, for the sake of his body the Church.'

True Fasting

When the bridegroom is taken away from them, that will be fasting indeed for the wedding guests.　(Luke 5:35)

What if we were to interpret every privation we feel, physical or emotional, as a real opportunity for expressing concretely our longing for the Bridegroom?

To accept the cold, monotonous food however it is served, lack of comforts . . . In all these things and others we are saying in an effective way: 'I long for the Bridegroom.'

This is what 'fasting' must be – the outward sign of a heart utterly sincere in its desire for God. Fasting from our own self-will, self-seeking – these are the practical ways in which we express our desire to be all for him.

To refrain from complaining or grumbling, to think nothing of anything that crosses us, is an expression of our longing for the Bridegroom – and one that captivates him.

Loving Others

In so far as you did this to one of the least of these brothers of mine, you did it to me. (Matthew 25:40)

'In the evening of life you will be examined on love.'

In the parable of the sheep and the goats Jesus makes it devastatingly clear that in the end it is only love of neighbour that counts – nothing else.

We shall not be examined on prayer, poverty, obedience or any of the other virtues; not because they are inessential but because they are real only insofar as we are wholly concerned with our neighbour.

You can't pray, obey, or be truly poor, says our Lord, unless you are wholly taken up with your brother's needs.

It is the 'least' we must be concerned with: this implies and demands the absence of all self-seeking, just unremitting devotion.

No human heart is capable of such devotion, but Jesus asks it because what is impossible to man is possible to God. He has identified himself with us completely – 'you did it, did it not . . . to me' – so that he may be our life.

What he asks we can therefore fulfil if we really want
   to,
if we pray from our hearts,
if we really take the trouble to do all we can do.

Forgiveness

How often must I forgive my brother?
(Matthew 18:21)

Perhaps the 'work' that best expresses faith is – forgiveness.

Jesus clearly saw that lack of forgiveness was one of the most blatant characteristics of the people around him, and he seemed to appreciate how hard it is to forgive absolutely and forever.

This is because we have no real grasp of what God has done and continually does for us.

Our lack of insight makes us critical, intolerant, unforgiving. We tend to think we have been splendid when we have taken a snub silently, overlooked what seemed like hurtful behaviour on the part of another.

It isn't like that at all, Jesus says. You are *bound* to have pity and to forgive. It isn't a work of supererogation but sheer bounden duty.

Think of the little things I take umbrage at, react to, or perhaps cope with quite virtuously according to my own estimation . . .

Now Jesus isn't saying: 'I understand, my poor dear; yes, you have been badly treated and you did very well not to lose your temper or answer back.'

On the contrary he is saying: 'It is unthinkable that you should take any notice whatever of such things, and you wouldn't if you had the slightest idea of what your heavenly Father is always doing for you. What if he were to treat you in that miserable, miserly, unloving way!'

Authority is Service

The teachers of the Law have sat in the chair of Moses, so you must obey everything they tell you. (Matthew 23:2)

Jesus tells his disciples unequivocally that they must obey lawful authority regardless of the defects of those in authority. He does not ask us to blind ourselves to these defects. He clearly recognized the immoral, irresponsible, unjust behaviour of those sitting in the chair of Moses.

He does not want any childish glorification of those in authority. He does not say they sit on the throne of God but in the chair of Moses, a human leader.

But it is God's will that we accept this law of human living which is that there be those in authority and those who obey for the common good.

In Jesus' eyes, human authority has a very lowly place: limited, without grandeur or fine titles, with no advantages whatever for the ones holding authority but only for those at whose service they are.

If we hold any sort of authority, either as an individual or as a group, we must avoid laying unnecessary burdens on those concerned. God never does this. His disciples must recognize their own dignity and refuse to offer cult or incense to any human authority.

Jesus wants every one of his disciples to be wholly detached from desire for human recognition, praise, status, popularity. If we want these things (as opposed to merely liking them) then we cut ourselves off from Jesus who wanted nothing but the Father's glory.

Only our grasp that we have a Father in heaven and a supreme Master in Jesus can enable us to live in our simple dignity without craving for false esteem.

Challenge and Response

The People of Nazareth

He slipped through the crowd and walked away.
(Luke 4:30)

We need divine help if we are to pass, with Jesus, from his enemies; from those who would destroy him.

These enemies lie within the heart of each one of us. To realize this we need light.

If we look at the Gospel of Luke, chapter 4, we see that the people of Nazareth were being offered light, light most painful to accept, and they rose in fury.

There is that within us that dreads the light, and it may well do so. This light carries with it a demand. There are other lights that cost nothing, rather they are delightful: happy reflections about God's love, about Jesus, about the Scriptures; they remain in the head.

The only light that matters is that which comes like a two-edged sword, and this the enemy within – which lurks in secret, hiding itself from our consciousness – resists with all its might. This enemy puts up a front as impenetrable as iron, and Jesus has no alternative but to turn away.

The actual demand the light makes may be small but of immense consequence, attacking something deep within us. We may be asked to let go once for all of a little animosity that still lies buried, a prejudice, a jealousy, to sacrifice our will in a particular instance . . .

Our deepest, most dangerous attachments we keep hidden – or rather, that enemy-self which is within, keeps them hidden from the self we *want* to know and *want* to claim.

Let us dare to pray for this fearful light. Fearful indeed, yet the compassionate God will cradle us in the pain and loneliness which such light always creates, as he cradled Jesus on the cross.

The Lawyer

Jesus said, 'You are not far from the kingdom of God.'
(Mark 12:34)

How little merely human insight avails!

This good lawyer speaks well of holy things and yet the comment of Jesus is that he is *not far* from the kingdom. He speaks high wisdom yet he is not *inside*, merely near. This should warn us not to overrate what we think we know of Jesus. All that matters ultimately is that we live it.

When we hear those great, solemn, beautiful words intoned – 'Listen O Israel . . . You must love the Lord your God with all your heart and all your soul, with all your mind and all your strength' – we can feel deeply moved. They resound in our soul as the very meaning of life.

But what are we actually doing to live out this totality of love which constitutes the very existence of Jesus himself?

The love of God is almost impossible to evaluate. Love of neighbour is the only guide to its existence, let alone its depths.

It is only in loving our neighbour that we can be set on loving God all the time and everywhere. There is no meaning to our human existence but this.

The more earnestly we want to surrender to God, the more determinedly we must work to love our neighbour.

The Rebellious Servants

We do not want this man to be our king.
(Luke 19:14)

At first sight this parable about the king and the servants who rejected him seems hardly relevant to us. *We* have accepted him gladly. But we must always look more deeply and ask ourselves in what way a parable, a teaching, calls us to judgement?

In each of us, in the very best of us, we have to admit sorrowfully that there is that which would have no part with him – that cries out, 'I do not want this man to be my king!'

If he came to us as the king of glory, if he came to us in a form we liked, then we would have him rule over us. But we know he has never come as the king of glory, and never will.

We see this was the life-long pressure against Jesus, his temptation – to meet the ungodly expectations of the people; to prove himself, to show himself by visible tokens of a worldly, not godly kind – to be *our* idea of the king of glory.

Rather than do this he was prepared to die. He willingly, consistently, chose the lowly, hidden, non-glorious path – right up to the end. 'Let him come down from the cross and we will believe.' The only answer is a cry of desolation.

Even his disciples, those whom he had sought out and

trained with special care, even these rejected him in his passion. He had to go on utterly alone. It was left to the most unlikely people to get just a glimpse of who and what he was. And the most astounding of all were the glimpses of some who saw him as he hung on the cross in human degradation. 'Indeed this was the son of God,' cried the centurion. 'Remember me, Jesus, when you come into your kingdom,' his companion besought him.

Now, he has singled us out with special love to be always with him, to be his special friends.

Unlike his first disciples we have hindsight. We know. We have the benefit of the experience and knowledge of the ages. Yet still we draw the line.

There are indeed many instances when we claim him as our king, but there is hardly one of us who does not draw the line somewhere; with some it is drawn much more quickly than with others. When something cuts us to the bone, then we find rationalizations to explain it away. This is not him . . . oh yes . . . this, this, this, that, that, that, . . . but not THIS.

We find it so hard to accept an uninteresting, non-exciting discipleship. We might recognize him in dramatic trials – but in the petty everyday? . . . how easily we say no. When we do, we are looking at the thorn-crowned, humiliated, helpless son of man and saying, 'We will not have him ruling over us, not that one!'

And for some of us, perhaps the hardest thing of all is to see him in our interior humiliations – in our shameful conflicts, contrary feelings, ugliness, depression.

Wherever there is lowly humanity . . . man in all his weakness, there is the Lord, there is the very Son of God ready to enfold us.

Dives and Lazarus

See that you never despise any of these little ones.
(Matthew 18:10)

Nothing matters in this life except to have loved God.

In the parable of Dives and Lazarus, Dives closed his heart to God. It was not because he was rich that he failed, but because he closed his heart to God before him in the other person.

The other person didn't matter to him; he didn't beat him or drive him off. He just ignored him because he was wrapped up in himself.

Our Lazarus need not be a pauper. Lazarus is merely the person who is not myself – the other – with his individuality and his own outlook and needs.

We need each other. None of us is truly rich, and sooner or later each of us suffers from ignoring the other. It is our mutual privilege to give to one another.

If I ignore a neighbour, undervalue him, judge him inferior, even in the most secret way, not only do I inflict wrong on him but I impoverish myself.

I must pray for the humility to realize that I need – and thus humbly hold out my little cup for the water of another whom, in my deepest heart, I have thought little of.

The Man at Bethzatha

Jesus saw him lying there and knew he had been in this condition for a long time. (John 5:6)

Whenever the Gospels put before us Jesus encountering an individual we are meant to say: 'That man, that woman is I', or at least some aspect of me.

This is true of the definitely unpleasant character depicted in the Gospel of John. He was a shirker, he was mean, sly . . .

Jesus points out to him his fundamental ill – you don't *want* to be healed, you don't want to make the effort. You expect it all to be done for you and when it isn't you are aggrieved and excuse yourself by throwing the blame on other people and circumstances.

Every one of us has that shirker within us who is a past-master at disguising the truth.

But then comes a moment of powerful grace – we see it, we can no longer hide the truth and we make an effort, a new beginning.

In the Gospel story Jesus is anxious about the man; he isn't content to let him be, sure of his continuing fidelity. He searches him out and confronts him, begging him to keep away from occasions of sin, to be infinitely serious and careful else he will be back where he was, and worse – because of the light he has received.

And there go we!

We allow ourselves to play again with whatever it was we had resolved against. We aren't serious enough, we don't want it enough.

It becomes a real betrayal of our Lord as, I think, we are meant to see in this Gospel story. The man knew Jesus was the object of hostility and was in danger. Angered by Jesus' challenge he points him out to his enemies and 'they began to persecute Jesus'.

We can never be neutral.

The Centurion

'Go home,' said Jesus, 'your son will live.'
(John 4:50)

At the very hour Jesus said, 'Your son will live,' it came about: the official's son was cured.

In our sacraments, Jesus works as powerfully as when he bade that boy live.

Our sacraments are ineffable – something human words cannot express. We recall the sacrament of the Eucharist, of Reconciliation, of the Sick, our Baptism which we renew on Easter night . . . These are the deep, sanctifying waters with which the Church, and indeed the whole world through the Church, is purified, reborn, made holy by being transformed into Christ.

In our sacraments we see no signs and wonders: nothing to compel assent. And yet in them we are confronted by Jesus directly in his healing, sanctifying power.

A sign made, a word spoken, 'Your son will live', and we have an absolute guarantee that he has laid his hand on us; his creative, restoring hand, bringing us to fullness of life.

Perhaps we could look at our attitude to the sacraments and test the sincerity and strength of our faith.

Mary of Bethany

Mary brought in a pound of very costly ointment.
(John 12:3)

Here we are shown a woman who was truly a disciple, one with a listening ear. She was a woman for whom Jesus really mattered, more than anything else in the world, more than herself.

She saw life's sole task as listening to the Lord, hearing the word of God, which always includes putting it into practice. We do not 'hear' in the biblical sense unless the hearing is translated into action. Like Martha, Mary too must have had many things to do but still only one sole purpose – to listen to the Lord.

The result was a deep knowledge of Jesus, of the hidden springs of his being, so to speak. As Jesus could say 'Holy Father the world has not known you, but I have known you' – because he lived on the Father's will, so this woman could say, 'Holy Jesus, the world has not known you, but I have known you.'

Thus she, of all others it seems, divined that he was to die and that this dying was his Father's will. She did not raise an outcry, or plan a campaign to stop him going to Jerusalem, nor did she attempt to dissuade him. She had entered into his deepest inner movements, no matter how dimly. She came with her symbolic gesture of pure devotion, identification, anointing him for his burial.

There is nothing else a disciple *can* do – no heroics, no glib professions that we are ready to die with him, but rather deep humility, deep gratitude for what *he* is doing. He has to do it in order to destroy our sin, our alienation from the Father. Then we shall be able to follow him.

Mary of Bethany is the symbol of Christian discipleship. If we do not come to this deep knowledge what does it mean? Yes, there is a Mary in us all, a devoted woman, but each of us has also to recognize a potential Judas, the worldling whose values are completely opposite to those of Jesus. Judas scorns the folly of the cross, the way of lowliness, humiliation, unimportance. He scorns the gesture of dumb, simple devotion. He is opposed to the mind of Christ who humbled himself, became nothing . . .

Judas too is capable of conversion. Ask our Lord with great earnestness to convert him wholly. Then there will be nothing in any of us but pure devotion – and the house will be filled with sweetness, refreshing the world.

A Listening Ear

My sheep listen to my voice, they will come to me.
(John 10:16)

God is always
at work in us,
prompting us to the good
and enabling us
to perform it.

'O that today
you would hear his voice.'

This constant listening
for his voice
demands
deep
sustained
self-denial.

Often we are occupied
in listening to ourselves . . .
our little grievances,
our petty wishes,
our mean desires.
We busy ourselves
with other peoples affairs
when they are
no business of ours.

While we live
in this manner
how can we tune in
to the Father's voice?

. . . . .

Jesus our brother
understands
our self-occupation.
Nevertheless
he goes on
exhorting us
to follow him,
to lay down
our own miserable lives
in order to live
by his abundant life . . .

. . . that
the works of God
might be displayed.

'Yes' in the Lord

Upholding all things by his word of power.
(Hebrews 1:3)

The word of power with which Jesus upholds the universe and bears it along to its fulfilment is his unequivocal and constant 'yes' to the Father and to his great plan for mankind.

Because of this 'yes' the Father is able to carry out all that he has promised.

Jesus gave his Father *carte blanche*. He could not see in detail the working of the plan. His life, like ours, was a multiplicity of choices whether in little things or great.

Not every occasion or demand bore on it the clear stamp of his Father's loving action. His 'yes' was often given in obscurity, bewilderment and pain. God had entrusted to his devoted servant the care of his family, sure that he would not fail them. On his frail, human shoulders was laid the burden of our destiny, a burden more precious to Jesus than all else.

There were times when it seemed unbearable: 'O faithless generation, how long am I to be with you? How long am I to bear with you?' What depths of loneliness and utter weariness in this forlorn cry! But he stayed with us and bore with us; he could not do other, for the Father's own love for us filled his human heart and eventually broke it open on the cross.

In his second letter to the Corinthians Paul says in his impassioned way: How could anyone who has seen the Lord, whom God has built up on the rock of Christ, has sealed as his own possession, who enhomes the Spirit, how can such a one vacillate between 'yes' and 'no'?* How can we let ourselves be governed by worldly standards, whether this pleases me or not, whether I like it or not, and so forth?

Of ourselves we would always vacillate, but we are empowered to be always 'yes,' and so to carry forward the great promises of God.

* 2 Cor. 1:18–22.

Sign of Contradiction

Just as Jonah became a sign . . .
(Luke 11:30)

Jonah in the belly of the whale. Why did this bizarre incident mean so much to Jesus? It held his attention, spoke deeply to his heart.

It is a very vivid illustration of what human life can be like, of what his own life was beginning to be like, and of the end he foresaw.

It means being tossed into an alien element where man, of himself, cannot live. There is nothing there that allows for what he understands as his own life.

This element, according to man's natural understanding, means destruction. And yet, as in the story of Jonah, we see that, in actual fact, it is the very encompassing of the Father in all his caring love, bringing him to life.

Jesus, in his response to the Jews' challenge for a sign, refuses every compromise, every reliance on what human reasoning, human power and experience can afford. He holds to one thing only – the Father's commitment to him, whatever the appearances to the contrary. This is the only sign he allows. How profound a lesson for us!

In surrendering to life as it unfolds no matter what it offers, in exposing ourselves to it – not evading, not fantasizing, not subtly (half consciously if not consciously) foreseeing things we don't want and warding them off, protecting ourselves in trying to control life – we are surrendered to the Father.

We must live with intense faith. And when we do this, we are acting like a secret radar, drawing safely into haven others who know him not and see in what happens only blind, cruel fate . . . Jonah in the belly of the whale.

Life's Only Meaning

Life is this: to know you, the only true God, and Jesus Christ whom you have sent. (John 17:3)

Each day of our lives holds within itself the possibility of this knowledge of God, this holy wisdom. How deeply we should long for this revelation of the Father.

Let us seek, let us listen with all our hearts and care for nothing else. Then perhaps we shall be able to exclaim with perfect truth: 'My heart knows you now, Jesus Christ my Lord, and everything worldly has lost its meaning.'

With perfect truth. That is, my life henceforth will reveal the truth that nothing has any meaning to me except Jesus Christ my Lord.

There is no easy way to this, only that the grain of wheat must die; the humble acceptance of our painful human lot; no complaint, no rebellion, no dodging . . . Becoming identified with the Son of Man, the sacrificial Lamb who takes away the sin of the world by bearing the full weight and effect of it with no vestige of responding evil – only worship of his Father and infinite compassion for us.

True Zeal

Run so as to win the prize.
(1 Corinthians 9:24)

St Paul likens our Christian life to a race, and he says that, though all run, only one obtains the prize.

That is strange, because we are quite certain that competition simply doesn't come into our living for God. Each one is called to win the prize.

What Paul is saying, I think, is that there is all the difference in the world between those who merely run – who like running, who are prepared to devote some time and energy to training, and yet who, fundamentally, go at their own pace – and the real athlete determined to win. And it is just the same in the Christian life.

Many indeed 'undertake it' as we say, and, it can be said in truth, work at it. But they lack that whole-hearted dedication essential if they are to attain the prize – complete union with God.

When my sister who had a weak heart was a child, the doctors said she could play games but never must she play in a match or run a race. Why? Because the determination to win would make her overstretch herself and could kill her.

But there is no fear of this happening in our living for God! In fact it is precisely this going all out that is essential. The non-dedicated runner will make certain sacrifices, put up with a certain amount of discipline, but sooner or later comes the decision, 'It isn't worth it.' Winning doesn't mean enough to him.

The one determined to win stops at nothing. The prize is worth it all. So must we live.

Let us ask ourselves if our living for God has this edge on it, this zeal, this unswerving passion?

Wholeheartedness

Anyone who loses his life for my sake will find it.
(Matthew 16:25)

The Christian life bears with it absoluteness, whole-heartedness, passion. The Church stands for this. An absolute affirmation, 'The Lord is God', and the concentration of all energy, all time, on him alone.

But we don't have to strain after some sort of appreci-ation of God, Infinite Being. No, we have been given the Way, the Truth, the Life in Jesus. We look at him and trust in him. We accept his vision of God. He has looked into the face of infinite Mystery and called It Father. He assures us by his very life-blood that It is utterly trustworthy. We ask for no other assurance than this. We do not ask to taste, to experience. We can make the leap of faith, we can determine to make him 'Father', our own God and our sole God.

But this is not the whole story. We are not left alone. We do not have to accomplish this leap in our own strength. This is quite impossible. God is helping us all along the way. He is communicating himself in light and love and courage, but we must do our part:

Firstly, we must constantly try to get to know our Lord by loving meditation on the Gospels, not relying merely on our own poor insights but making use of the best commentaries. This application must never come to an end.

Secondly, there must go with this a corresponding effort to put his teaching into practice.

And sustaining both these efforts and accompanying them must go continual prayer for light and strength to know God and to love him.

Each activity must keep pace with the other. Not one of the three may lag behind the others. This is our indispensable part and is the 'active' element in our ascent of the mountain of God.

When we see what God is, when we see the heaven and earth that he has made, what can we do but adore?

It is the Lord your God you must worship, and give yourself to him, body and soul.

All for God

Happy are your eyes because they see, your ears because they hear! (Matthew 13:16)

We must resolve to put the whole of our sense life at God's service. We must refuse to use our senses except when their exercise is for the honour and glory of God.

We can so easily presume that the whole bent of our being is to God, and fail to recognize how we allow ourselves dangerous distractions; how we allow ourselves to notice and nose into other people's business; how we yield to useless curiosity, indulge ourselves in countless ways.

Hold up! Fix your eyes on the perfect Son. Hold yourself in your hands so that your activities are controlled, that you know what you are doing, and are not drifting by carelessly occupied with trifles, occupied with yourself.

Our whole way of life should be helping us to this true recollection, this concentration on God. Sustained discipline is absolutely essential if we are to belong to God.

'Many prophets and holy men longed to see what you see and never saw it, to hear what you hear, and never heard it.' Let's weigh these words.

How utterly privileged we are to know Christ Jesus our Lord. How privileged to have access to his words, his thoughts . . . Do we really see this as an unheard-of privilege? We shall answer that question truthfully by looking at what we do. Are we always most seriously, with everything we have in us, trying to get to know him and trying to live according to his teaching?

. . . The torch is sweeping slowly round our room. Do we want to see the cobwebs? Do we want to remove them? Or do we allow our eyes to rest on them for a brief moment only, and then go on just as before.

Ever Present

True worshippers will worship the Father in spirit and truth. (John 4:23)

Outward worship of itself avails nothing. We have to pay attention, apply our minds to God's service: the whole of ourselves must be brought to bear on our loving service of him. This cannot be done without great labour.

Day by day, hour by hour, we must be renewing the offering of ourselves, making sure it is not a matter of words and sentiments, but actuality. Everything we do, from morning to night, must be truthful, coming from our deepest centre.

How few of us, says St Thérèse, always do our best, never take little holidays but *always* are attentive to God, present to him, waiting on him, loving him.

This is the living sacrifice, holy and acceptable, the pure spiritual worship which alone matters to him.

Gift and Witness

If only you knew the gift of God.
(John 4:10)

We bear
a tremendous responsibility
for one another.
Each of us
is a minister
of Christ.
Each of us
has to witness
to him.
Everything we do,
        say,
          or even think
has either a positive
or a negative
effect on others.

Nothing is neutral.
Bad example,
carelessness about faults,
lack of charity;
all these things
affect
the purity
and love
of a community.
And
following from that
weaken the charity
of the whole Church.

St Paul entreats us
not to trifle
with the precious grace
of God.
This grace,
which is nothing less
than God
offering himself
is available
      NOW.
        NOW is the acceptable time
        NOW is the significant time.

If we had
a lively faith,
grasped this fact,
we would indeed
give no offence –
put no obstacle
in another's way

Do not trifle
with the precious gift
of God.

The Apostolate of Prayer

My Father goes on working.
(John 5:17)

The Father is the vine-dresser pruning his vine. This pruning entails a very great purification of the self. We must allow this to happen, surrender ourselves with Jesus to the Father's loving action.

We must look around the world, not only in the present, but down into past ages, and see the multitudes living out their lives with no knowledge of him, no reference to him; what St Peter calls 'a useless way of life'.

Yet every one of this innumerable multitude has been ransomed every bit as much as we have. Each one has been bought with a great price and is continually receiving redemption – though they know it not.

We Christians are called to be priests of this vast multitude. We *know* the name of the Lord; we praise him; we celebrate his love and goodness, and the great act by which our redemption was accomplished. And we do this for ALL.

We do it daily in our Mass, in our prayer, in our lives. We know the inmost heart of the Paschal Mystery. It is the mystery in which the whole creation finds its meaning – from which it comes, to which it goes. We tap its wellsprings and, so to speak, cause them to flow more abundantly over the face of the earth, into the hearts of all men.

It isn't just a matter of mental application and trying to evoke suitable emotional responses to the celebration of the Paschal Mystery, but a profound, living desire to be conformed to it. We must want all the Father has longed and longs to do for us to be accomplished in our own hearts.

'It has pleased God to reveal his Son in me.' We should desire that this be true in the fullest way. For God to reveal his Son in me, there must be nothing in me but Jesus.

This is the only true apostolate – which goes to the very roots of human existence and sanctifies them. A wholly hidden apostolate.

'In the Father's eyes nothing is pleasing in anyone living or dead, but his likeness to Jesus!'

Trustful and Forgiving

Your Father knows what you need before you ask him.
(Matthew 6:8)

Central to all Jesus' teaching is that we have a Father in heaven. This must influence us in everything.

When we pray we do not resort to magic formulae, to a spate of prescribed words. We speak to our Father from our hearts.

Do not babble . . . God only hears what the heart is saying. If the words are empty, devoid of true longing there is no prayer.

What a word of endless comfort, 'Your Father knows' – every syllable precious; but a word too of absolute demand – 'Your Father knows . . . but *you* do not.'

Prayer is not a matter of telling God our needs, but of allowing him to tell us; and he tells us in the Lord's Prayer. Our all-embracing need is that his kingdom should come in us; that everything in us should be wholly conformed to his will.

Then he picks out one specific requirement for this to be so. 'Forgive us as we forgive.'

To refuse forgiveness means our Father will not forgive us. To forgive others their failings is to be forgiven by our Father.

God will not forgive us if we do not forgive. Will not because he cannot. His love cannot penetrate a heart that has hardened itself. Deep-seated resentments, bitterness, these petrify the heart and block every prayer we utter.

'Your Father in heaven will not forgive you, unless each one, from the depths of his heart, pardons and embraces his brother.'*

* Matt. 6:14.

With Jesus in his Passion

I Lay Down my Life

The Father loves me because I lay down my life . . . for my sheep. (John 10:17)

Jesus is saying that the Father is seized with love, admiration, gratitude to him because he lays down his life fully. Why should the Father be so enamoured of this act of Jesus laying down his life, accepting to die?

In the first place because the Father can only find an outlet for his love when a human creature consents to die to his own limited, merely natural life.

The condition for being transformed into God's likeness, for entering into his own dimension is – being ready to go beyond ourselves, allowing ourselves to be taken away from self, consenting to leave the limitations of our merely natural being.

This acceptance of dying has to be done in the dark, in blind trust in the promise of the Father.

The dimension into which we are called is 'God': so 'other', so mysterious as to be beyond thought or imagination; and therefore, in a sense, meaningless to us.

We live a caterpillar existence and are completely incapable of conceiving of a butterfly existence. It is an awful thing to be told – or rather asked – to be willing to die to our caterpillarness in order to be something we have no notion of and no desire for.

We like being caterpillars – we have cabbage leaves to feed on, our world is circumscribed and manageable, it's solid. 'What's all this about a new way of being . . . ? Flitting about in the air . . . ? No thanks – I'd rather be as I am!'

God's agonizing struggle is to get his human creatures to love and trust him enough to make the decision, to accept to die to their caterpillar life . . . It does seem like a tomb, that dark cocoon; no activity worth calling activity . . . a death to all we understand at present of life.

But Jesus accepted. This is the great triumph. He accepted, with all the adoring love of his heart, to lay down his life. This act was his supreme expression of the greatness of his love for his Father – that he, the Father, mattered alone, and that all Jesus wanted was to do his will, and to allow the Father to do in him and through him whatever he pleased.

And it is then God's good pleasure to fill his creature with blessings.

To Jerusalem and Death

What do you think? Will he come to the festival or not?
(John 11:56)

Most certainly he will come to the festival; most certainly he will come to Jerusalem to celebrate the Pasch, to establish the eternal festival. He will walk into the lion's mouth, to a certain death, because his Father wills him to proclaim his message in the capital at the solemn feast.

There is no equivocation in Jesus: no 'yes' and then 'no', but always a most emphatic 'yes'. There is no equivocation either in his enemies, they are determined to kill him.

It is the common people and even the disciples who equivocate: What think you about him? will he come? is he to be trusted? . . . and so on. A lot of talk, speculation, playing about with the idea of him, but basic frivolity and lack of commitment.

We are like that at least to some extent. We stand by him in verbal affirmation and in liturgical ceremony, but each of us has to examine how far our actual commitment squares with what we profess.

We are committed – up to a point,
we follow him – up to a point,
but have not yet cast ourselves, absolutely, irrevocably,
onto his side.

Think about it: those seemingly small but pernicious criticisms, those quick retorts expressive more of our indignation and aggrieved pride than of pure love, that allowing of resentful thoughts and feelings, playing with mistrust, depression, discouragement, instead of a loyal rejection of such things.

God's grace is always flowing plentifully. Each morning there are special outpourings. Let us determine that today will see an end of our equivocation and the beginning of an unswerving discipleship.

Let us go to die with him.

Preparing the Pasch

Where is the room in which I am to eat the Paschal meal with my disciples? (Luke 22:11)

Our Lord is saying this to each one of us now, 'I wish to celebrate my Pasch at your house with my disciples.' He wants to accomplish in us his dying and his rising; he wants us completely identified with him in his perfect sacrifice.

We, the Church, are the little flock to whom it is given to know the name of the Lord and thereby to praise that name – and we do it *on behalf of all*. We can be sure that there are countless people going about their daily tasks, occupied with this world, in whom our Lord is able to celebrate his Pasch, but they do not know it. We to whom he is a living Love, who consciously open ourselves to his redemption, consciously pray to receive the fullness of his love, always do this for others.

You are the light of the world, the salt . . . the yeast . . . for others.

We should have it deeply at heart that the Church be purified of all worldliness, be made truly pure, holy, loving, be indeed the light of the world. And we begin at home, in our own hearts.

In Mark's Gospel we are told that Jesus expressed his unutterable grief, 'I am dying of sorrow.' What an expression! What precisely was his grief? He did not say he was dying of fear though he was feeling fear.

No, it was grief that was killing him. For what? Perhaps we find the clearest answer in Luke: 'Seeing the city he wept over it, *If only* you had known . . .'

Perhaps we can say his passion of grief was to see us refusing so much love, so much happiness; choosing to remain trapped in our misery. No affronted dignity, no self-pitying hurt at his love being rejected, but grief for the misery of those he loved. He had come to rescue them from the pit but they preferred to stay in it. The obdurate hardness of man's heart!

And we must always remember that what is taking place in Jesus' heart is the human reflection of what is happening in God.

Reflecting on this grief, shouldn't we want to make it our sole desire to do the only thing we can – open our hearts fully to redeeming love?

'Accomplish love to your full satisfaction in me.'

When this is so, the very love of Jesus takes possession of our hearts and we too shall find ourselves concerned only with the work of God, devoid of self-interest. 'Come, Master, celebrate your Pasch in my house – I open its doors wide to you.'

The Hour of Redemption

Father the hour has come, glorify your Son.
(John 17:1)

Night has fallen. The terrible sin – that of killing the Lord – the epitome of all sin, is as good as accomplished. And Judas goes off . . .

Night has fallen indeed and yet, within the supper room there is a cry of exultation that is, in itself, a shattering of the night. 'The hour has come for the Son of Man to be glorified.'

Jesus is to die, and he accepts this with all the passionate commitment of his surrendered heart – so deep, so unrestricted is his love for us. His is Love to the end, the uttermost love, which is total self-expenditure.

He knows that the love driving him on is not born of the human spirit; he knows that the Father himself is pouring into his poor human heart the immensity of his own self-expending love for men.

When he hangs on the cross, naked, emptied out, reduced to nothing, we shall have some idea of what this Man is, who he is, Son of eternal Love itself. Looking on him, seeing him truly for the first time, we shall know what sort of a God we have; for the first time human beings will know what God is really like.

He is a complete reversal of all merely human notions of God: he is Love that gives.

We wounded him by our sinning – we bruised him –
yet all he bore became our healing.

Eucharistic Self-Giving

Shall I not drink the chalice my Father gives me?
(John 18:11)

Let us dwell on that last evening of our Lord's mortal life – the supper. Nothing is left to Jesus at this hour but himself. He stands amid the ruins of what he tried to do, what he thought he had to do. And he has failed. The people have not listened.

The chosen few whom he had hoped would be the new people of God, upon whom he had lavished all that he had, do not believe. They will all run away. Even now one of them is betraying him. Is there even *one* on earth who really understands? Who has received or entered into the Kingdom? Is there one single thing he can point to or hold onto as a guarantee that he has achieved something, fulfilled his appointed task? No. And yet, 'My heart has not wavered, O God, my heart has not wavered.'

He has come to realize that the kingdom *has* come in his own perfect, unswerving obedience to the Father; in *his* total acceptance of life which, he understands, always flows from the hands of the Father, no matter what the material, personal channels. He, Jesus, in his perfect acceptance and surrender *is* the kingdom. He has nothing else to offer but his own pure heart.

Therefore he is glad to die in failure, in loneliness, as a supreme testimony of love, obedience and trust. 'Father, the world has not known You, but I have known You.' He is determined that the Father should have it all – no matter what the cost. In blind faith, consistent to the end, he sees life flowing from the Father's hand.

And so his terrible betrayal, his bitter death at the hands of cruel men is 'the chalice my Father gives me', to be drained with all the passionate love and devotion of his heart.

In profound peace he seals his self-offering with a ritual gesture: 'Take and eat, this is my body – for you . . . Take and drink the new Covenant in my blood . . . Do this that the Father remember me.' This alternative rendering, considered authentic, rings in my own heart as authentic. Jesus *never* sought himself.

Rembrandt's picture of Jesus breaking bread at Emmaus seems to be a perfect portrayal of the Saviour. The Lord is lowly, suffering, insignificant. There is no drama or bombast, just a quiet, loving dedication, the grandeur of which was hidden even from himself. 'She has done what she could.' These words echo his own lowly self-estimation – 'I have done what I could.'

As daily we receive from those holy hands his sacrificed, surrendered self, he longs to draw us into his unswerving self-offering to the Father.

If he is to have his way, we too must live in perfect obedience, accepting life in all its details – and that includes our selves, our heredity and temperament – as from the Father. It is 'the chalice which my Father gives me', to be drained without rebellion, evasion, complaint.

Simple, yes, but demanding our full attention and all our energy.

I Go to the Father

Now has the Son of Man been glorified.
(John 12:23)

Does Jesus' cry rise up from vision, from beatific joy? Not at all. It is remarkable how often in the Gospels, considering their non-emotional nature, mention is made of Jesus' grief, weeping, distress, perturbation – human reactions to human situations. And this is found in John's Gospel most of all.

We are told that Jesus was deeply distressed. And then comes his magnificent cry: 'Now has the Son of Man been glorified.' This cry is pure faith. His senses are pressing him down, but his spirit exults in God his saviour. He can echo Isaiah:

> The Lord God is my helper
> and that help cannot play me false . . .
> I know well that I cannot suffer
> the shame of defeat.
> One stands by me
> to vindicate my cause.

89

Is there one who
makes his way through darkness
with no glimmer of light?
Then let him trust in the Lord
and lean upon his God.

What is actually happening to Jesus now *is* his resurrection. As he surrenders himself more and more totally, the Father fills him. What breaks forth when the mortal bonds are broken is what has been growing there all the time, and now reaches completion.

'You cannot follow me now,' says Jesus. This journey is Jesus' own, no one has trod it before. Only when he has made it can we also follow. And how in this life?

Jesus gives the answer: Show the world what I am, by loving one another as I love you – total expenditure of self for others, handing over of self continually.

Thus his disciples reveal him and his Father. Thus are they being slowly born into his risen life.

The Promise of Resurrection

I shall go before you to Galilee.
(Matthew 26:32)

Jesus is the pioneer of our faith. We need to look at him to learn what faith really is – what it means to trust, to believe.

He was on his way to the garden as his life drew to its close when he spoke those words: 'I shall go before you into Galilee.'

He was facing death; his mission seemingly cut short abruptly with nothing whatever achieved. Desertion by his own chosen followers was the ultimate failure . . . not even these believed and were prepared to stake their all on him.

He stands among the ruins, with not a shred of human hope or assurance, with no sign coming from above, with nothing but the witness of his own heart. ('I know the Father, and were I to deny that I know him I would be a liar, and knowing him I know he will ultimately triumph. He will never let me down. I have come at his word, on his mission; I have always done what pleased him and now, in this dark, empty hour I trust him utterly. Father, I place my life in your loving hands.')

Because he is standing, not in his own fragile self but in the fathomless ocean of the Father's love, he can forget himself even as he bends over the brink, staring into the dark depths of the agony awaiting him. His concern is for his friends whom, he foresees, are soon to desert him shamefully. His concern is to console them, to infuse them with his own faith and trust.

Yes, he will soon be drinking wine again with them, but then the Kingdom will have come! He will be meeting them in Galilee as of old and yet so differently! *Then* they will *see* him. They fail now because they do not see him, have never seen him; but soon, very soon, they are to see him, and their hearts will be full of joy that will never, never fail.

We need to look at Jesus. And looking at him we draw a sweet breath of pure forgiveness and the pure hope it brings.

'You fail me, you let me down, but it doesn't matter now. The Father puts all things right. Trust him, trust me. Meet me with joy in Galilee.'

Concluding Prayer

Jesus, holy and beloved
hold me always in your 'yes'.
Let nothing matter to me from this moment
but the Father's good pleasure,
the coming of his kingdom.
Let me not matter to myself.
I have only one short life in which to love
in difficulty and pain,
trusting in the dark and non-seeming.
Opportunities come and pass forever,
never to return.
Let me not miss one,
let my life be lived in total love:

There is no other way of living a truly human life.

Maranatha

When the corn is green
    the blackbird singing
My love will come
    swift as a fountain springing,
Will seize me
    hold me
    clasp me to him
    bringing
        infinite gladness.